IMAGES
of England

SCUNTHORPE'S INDUSTRIES

Maxmilian Mannaberg, the man who brought steel to Scunthorpe.

IMAGES
of England

SCUNTHORPE'S
INDUSTRIES

Compiled by
Reg and Peter Cooke

Gold is for the mistress; Silver for the maid
Copper for the craftsman, cunning at his trade.
'Good', cried the Baron sitting in his Hall,
'But iron, cold iron, is master of them all.'

Rudyard Kipling

TEMPUS

First published 1999
Copyright © Reg and Peter Cook, 1999

Tempus Publishing Limited
The Mill, Brimscombe Port,
Stroud, Gloucestershire, GL5 2QG

ISBN 0 7524 1634 0

Typesetting and origination by
Tempus Publishing Limited
Printed in Great Britain by
Midway Clark Printing, Wiltshire

We dedicate this book to Kathleen,
a wife and mother,
whose patience and encouragement
supported us throughout the compilation

Wives and children taking meals to the workers at Frodingham Ironworks. c.1905.

Contents

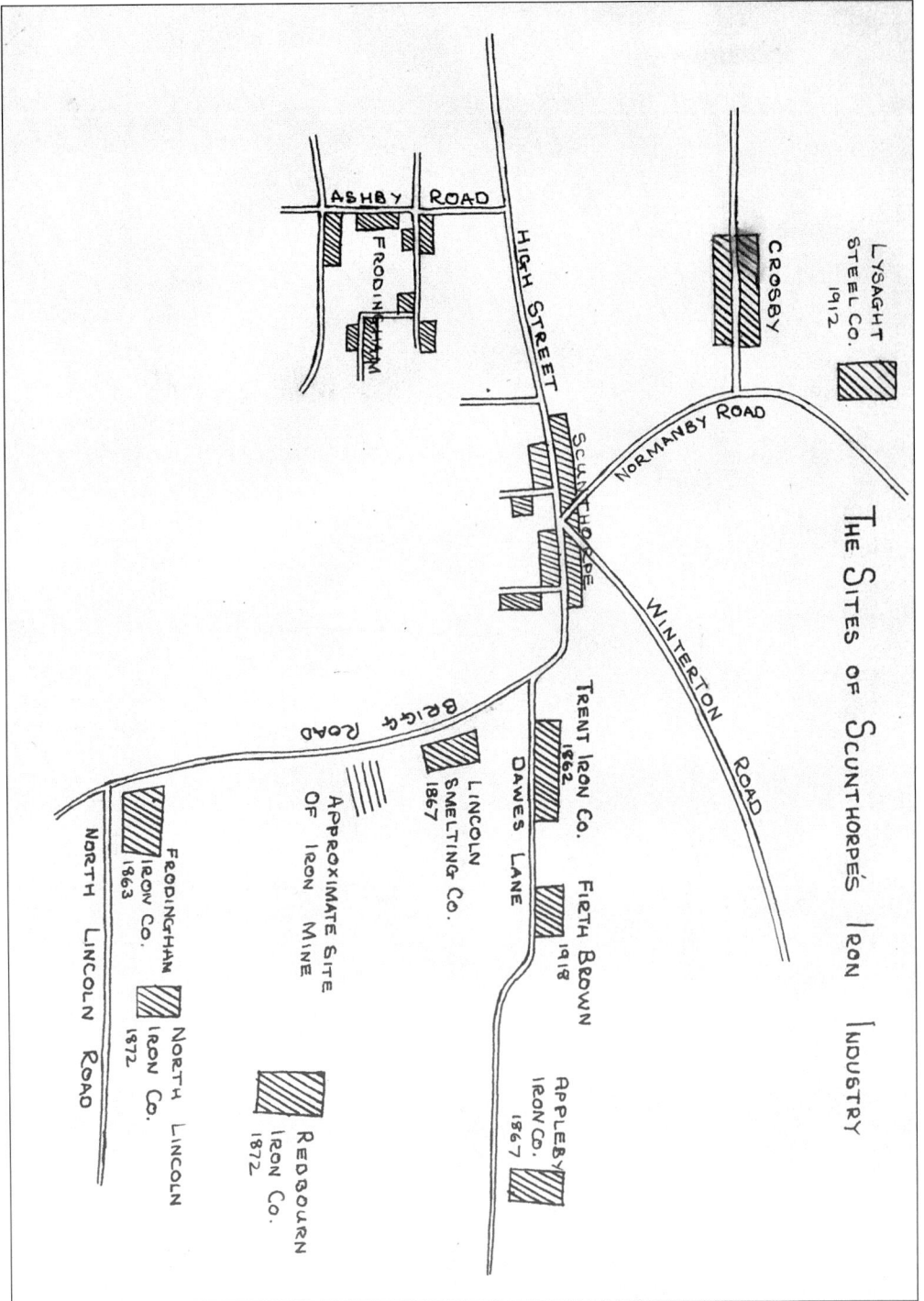

A sketch map showing the sites of Scunthorpe's iron industry, drawn by the late Jim Coley.

Foreword

During the twentieth century technological and industrial progress has arguably been the most rapid that will ever be experienced. Within a single generation the concept of motor car was soon surpassed by man's conquest of flight and, subsequently, the exploration of space.

Throughout this period of advancement, photography has played a vital role, as a research and investigative aid, as a scientific tool and as a means of capturing images of occasions, developments and, above all, people, for historic records. Cameras and photographic materials have constantly improved and today, with the availability of video and electronic imaging technology, the opportunity to obtain pictorial records for future generations is available to everyone like never before. I have spent almost forty years in the business of gathering pictures for hundreds of purposes. For most of this time I have known Reg Cooke and have been impressed with his painstaking efforts to collate a wealth of photographs depicting life in Scunthorpe over many decades. Amongst this collection he has accumulated possibly the most comprehensive selection of historic pictures covering the development of the Iron and Steel Industry in the town.

The changing skylines, the transition from hard, demanding manual work to modern hi-tech production methods and the people involved in this dramatic transformation are all represented in this publication. I am sure that many memories of the past will be brought to life again as you browse through these pages.

Knowing of his tireless efforts to preserve such a gold mine of history I feel privileged to write this preface and to recommend this work to you. I know that many of you will be enthralled by Reg Cooke's knowledge of so many of the characters and events which have played such an important part in the development of Scunthorpe's iron and steel industry.

Gordon K. Davison
Video Production and Photographic Services Manager,
British Steel.

Scunthorpe's famous 'Four Queens' blast furnaces at South Ironworks.

Acknowledgements

Our grateful and sincere thanks go out to the people of Scunthorpe who, over the years, have allowed us to copy their precious photographs. To Kathleen, for her patience and moral support, and for putting up with our untidiness and neglect of the garden and house during the process of compilation. To all the local photographers, past and present, who have recorded our history so extensively. To Reg Henry, Fred Cooke, Graham Donald, Roy Featherstone, Alec Smith and everyone else who has provided special insight. To all of our friends and family for their endless love and support over the years. And finally, our deepest gratitude to British Steel's Scunthorpe Works and especially to Gordon Davison, Chris Mimmack, and David Davis of British Steel's Video Section and Photographic Department for their encouragement and support over many years.

One

Mining

The re-discovery of ironstone was recorded by the late Harold Dudley, the founder and curator of Scunthorpe's first museum, from an interview with an old resident, William Skinner. 'When Scunthorpe was a village, we carted rubbly ironstone, which we called Marl, onto the land to kill a weed called Maiden's Hair. The rough stone was burnt into lime and if too much coal was used the stone melted and turned into clinkers. One day, in 1859, Charles Winn, who had been awarded the sandy commons to the east of Scunthorpe under the Enclosures Act, stopped with his shooting party near a lime clamp, as these kilns were called. One of the party picked up a clinker and said that he thought that it was ironstone.' Mr Winn sent for George Dawes and John Rosebury, who visited the site and confirmed the presence of ironstone. The beginning of heavy industry had arrived.

John Rosebury stayed as the mining manager for the Winn family, and George Dawes, along with his brother, bought ironstone for their Elsecar, Denby Dale and Milton Works in the Rotherham area. The first ore was mined in July 1860 from areas approximately at the Old Courthouse and the east wing of the current Frodingham administration building. This spread westwards towards Manley Street and up to St Johns Church area. This area was finally mined out in the early 1900s. The area to the east of Frodingham, as far as Brigg Road, was mined out by 1892. Mining spread eastwards, then north and south. The ironstone ran out of quality at Ashbyville but continued northwards.

In 1958 Winterton Quarry was opened upon the Dip Face of Coleby Ironstone Co. to feed Redbourn Works. During the following six summers, a large Roman Villa was excavated on the site. One of the mosaic pavements found now forms the entrance wall of the Civic Centre.

Most of the ore was accessible by opencast mining with the overburden being removed by hand to open up the ironstone seam. This was done by men called 'Sanders' who filled their barrows and walked over two 11in planks, each resting side by side on trestles, to dump the soil away from the ironstone bed. This was a very dangerous job, and was carried out in all weathers. The trestles could be up to 30ft above ground, and, whilst the Sanders could position themselves astride the two planks, the barrow wheel had to be in the centre of just one of the planks making it difficult to balance.

The Sanders, sometimes called Barers, worked twelve-hour shifts and were paid by the cubic yard. In 1900 they were paid twopence halfpenny (about 1p) per cubic yard of sand and fourpence halfpenny plus 15% for clay, with a figure between for soil. The overburden was split into 'benchings', an area for each Sander to work and a cubic foot of overburden weighed around 1.5 tons.

The men who loaded the ironstone were called 'Chuckers' and their pay in 1900 was also twopence halfpenny per ton but they had to buy their own blasting powder and fuses. In 1860 they were only paid one farthing a ton (one tenth of 1p). The Chuckers were not expected to lift lumps of more than ninety-six pounds!

Mechanization came into Winn's Mines in 1885, with the use of steam shovels for removal of overburden, but the other companies continued with the old method. Horses were used extensively and were still in use in the 1920s.

The first underground mine shafts were sunk around 1870, but it was not until 1939, when the Santon Mine opened, that serious underground mining started.

In December 1988 local ore mining ceased, as the use of richer foreign ores became normal practice.

Sanders removing overburden with ironstone Chuckers working on the seam.

Sanders working in Trent Mines in the 1930s.

A view of the trestles used by the Sanders to cross the mine. Note the Sander tipping material into the wagon from a height of about 36ft without any safety measures at all.

Left: Hand mining in Yarborough Mine. The overburden is removed by barrow over a trestle bridge while the ironstone Chuckers fill the waggons.
Right: Sanders with heavily loaded barrows crossing planks. Note the way the wheel of the barrow is positioned in the centre of just one plank.

Ironstone Chuckers at work on the iron seam. The depth of the overburden is clearly visible.

A team of ironstone Chuckers. Note the shape of their shovels.

Mechanization in the Mines in the early 1900s. A steam-crane is removing the overburden and feeding it onto the transporter, while another steam-crane is mining the ironstone and filling wagons.

A closer view of similar machinery at work.

A very early steam-shovel at work on the overburden.

141.

A steam-shovel filling the wagons of the loco *Alexandra*, 10 April 1917.

A German-made Lubecker Chain-Bucket Excavator-Dredger at Ashbyville, *c.*1912.

A Ransomes & Rapier Walking Dragline removing overburden at Yarborough Mine, 18 October 1956.

Walking Drag-lines at work removing overburden in the Yarborough Mines in 1965. The Redbourn Works and North Ironworks can be seen in the background.

Goosehole Mine, c.1903.

Core-drilling at the Yarborough
Mine, 19 December 1958.

Midland Ironstone Company's
Saddletank loco *Julia Sheffield*.

Pneumatic drilling for explosive planting at Yarborough Mines, c.1950. Note the two gasholders of Redbourn and North Ironworks in the background.

The J. Sullivan T2 Drill. Dragonby Mines, March 1951.

Two

The first to rise – the first to fall

Trent, North Lincoln and Lindsey Ironworks

The first ironworks to be built in Scunthorpe was the Trent Ironworks of the brothers W.H. & G. Dawes. It was situated down Wheatlands, which was later named Dawes Lane after them. Originally, they transported their mined ore to their Elsecar, Denby Dale and Milton Works. It was taken by horse and cart down to the river Trent and then shipped by barge from Chatterton's Wharf near Neap House. In time, the horse track got so rutted that the wagons sank to their axles. They overcame this by building a rail track using horses to pull the wagons.

On 26 March 1864 Trent's first furnace was blown-in. It was filled with 420 tons of local stone, thirteen tons of foreign ore and sixty-seven tons of flue, thought to be tap cinder from puddling furnaces. The blast furnaces were 40ft high with a 14ft bosh.

The Trent Ironworks were demolished in 1935 as part of a national rationalization of the iron industry.

North Lincoln Ironworks was the third ironworks to be built, and it worked from 1866 to 1929. North Lincoln purchased ore from Winn's Mines, unlike Trent who mined their own on land leased from Winn. In 1922 the works were purchased by Stewart & Lloyds. They were going to build an iron and steel works on the site but they changed their minds and built at Corby instead. The works fell into disrepair and was bought by Appleby Frodingham Works in 1931, who built coke ovens on the site when South Ironworks was built in 1938.

The Lincolnshire Iron & Smelting Co. Ltd was the fifth works to be built and produced their first iron in November 1873. They were purchased by the Redbourn Hill Iron & Coal Co. Ltd in 1883 and renamed Lindsey Works. They became an embarrassment, as Redbourn Works were in financial difficulties, and were blown up in 1905.

In 1862 work began to build the first ironworks in Scunthorpe: the Trent Ironworks of Dawes Bros.

Trent Ironworks' blast furnaces viewed from the railway lines. The first cast of iron was on 26 March 1864.

William Dixon, Keeper at Trent Ironworks in the 1920's, tapping the blast furnace. He was the great and great-great-grandfather of the compilers.

A sketch of Trent Ironworks produced for an illuminated address (see pages 89-93).

Trent Ironworks from St John's Church tower.

Trent Ironworks cottages.

Above and below: Two different views of the demolition of Trent Ironworks in 1935. Trent Ironworks was the first to rise and the first to fall.

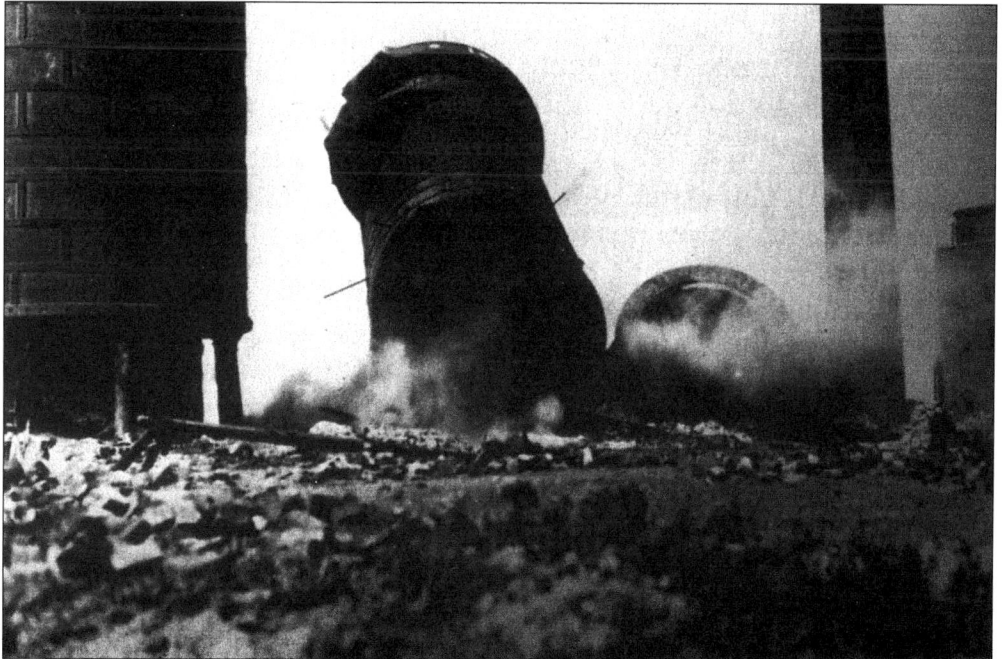

Lindsey Ironworks. Trent Ironworks cottages can be seen in the background.

LINDSEY WORKS THE EXPLOSION.

Blowing up buildings at Lindsey Ironworks, 1905.

Preparation for the demolition of the chimney at Lindsey Ironworks.

Right: Dropping the chimney.

*Following pages:*A general view of North Lincoln Ironworks, *c.*1925.

The North Lincoln Ironworks blast furnaces.

The North Lincoln Blast House, looking towards Redbourn Cathedral building and blast furnaces.

Three
Redbourn Works

In 1872 two small hand-charged blast furnaces were blown in at the Redbourn Hill Iron & Coal Co. Ltd Works. These were later rebuilt and the works enlarged. In 1925 the interests of the Redbourn Hill Iron & Coal Co. Ltd were wound up, and the assets transferred to Richard Thomas & Co. Ltd. Prior to this, during the First World War, work started on a fourth blast furnace and steel works. The first steel furnaces were commissioned in October 1918 and first cast at the end of November.

The Rolling Mill commenced operation about the middle of the 1920s. After the 1920s recession, trade picked up and Redbourn saw major developments in 1933 when two more open hearth steel furnaces were added, making seven in all. In the same year, the Whitehead Thomas Bar & Strip Mill was dismantled from Whitehead's Tredegar Works and rebuilt at Redbourn Works.

A new brick works was built in 1936 at Belton to supply Redbourn with bricks. No.3 Coke Oven Battery was built in 1938 and the scrapping of the old, smaller type of locomotive began. They were replaced by more up-to-date and powerful ones ready to pull larger slag ladles when the future enhancement of the Blast Furnaces was completed. This was a slow programme and was completed in 1950.

Redbourn became part of the Richard Thomas & Baldwin Group in 1944 when Richard Thomas merged with Baldwins.

In 1951 two hand-charged blast furnaces were demolished while a new mechanically charged one was built. The final skyline was three almost identical blast furnaces.

In 1961 a rotor furnace for pre-refining hot steel was built and in 1962 the SACK Bloom Mill began operation.

On 8 September 1980 the blast furnaces at Redbourn were blown up, iron making having ceased in 1979. The Sinter Plant continued to supply sinter to Queen Mary and Queen Bess Blast Furnaces at South Ironworks until December 1988, when Redbourn Works finally closed down.

The Redbourn blast furnaces, *c.*1880.

The Redbourn blast furnace crew, 1882. Note the young children who were employed.

The Redbourn Ironworks in full operation at the start of its life.

Removing slag ladles from Redbourn blast furnaces.

The Redbourn blast furnaces, August 1974. Showing of a slag ladle in the foreground.

Demolition of the Redbourn blast furnaces in September 1980.

Clugstons slag works with Redbourn blast furnaces and Appleby gasholders on the skyline.

Charging open-hearth furnaces at Redbourn.

Hand-charging of the Redbourn soaking pits, before they changed to gas-fired operation.

Building of the Redbourn Rotor furnace. This furnace was commissioned in 1961 and was the first of its kind in the country.

Charging molten iron into the Redbourn Rotor furnace.

The Redbourn Sack Blooming Mill, which was erected during the closure period in August and September 1962.

The Whitehead-Thomas Bar and Strip Mill, c.1965.

The Redbourn Sketch Shears.

A view of the Redbourn Coke Ovens.

An overall view of the Redbourn Works.

Four
Normanby Park Works

The only works to be built in Scunthorpe as a fully integrated iron and steel works was the Normanby Park Works of John Lysaghts & Co. Ltd Work, commenced in 1911. It came on stream in 1912.

Normanby Park Works was always known locally as Lysaghts even after it changed ownership.

Initially, it had three blast furnaces, (a further two were added in 1915 and a sixth one in 1960) and four open-hearth steel furnaces. It also had one mixer to supply 2,000 tons of ingots per week to a 36in Cogging Mill and a 32in Finishing Mill.

During the First World War, Lysaghts provided the steel to Foster and Co. of Lincoln to build their 'water tanks for Mesopotamia'. This was the code name given to the project to build the new war machine – the Dreadnought Tank.

John Berry Group took over the interests in the company which, in 1922, was bought by Guest Keen & Nettleford, after first becoming associated with Joseph Sankey & Sons of Bilston.

A major enhancement programme was carried out in 1930 comprising the first new coke oven battery in the country to be fired by blast furnace gas, a crushing plant, a gasholder and two new steel furnaces with ancillary plant.

In 1937 a two pan Greenawalt Sinter Plant was built. A third pan was added in 1945. They were taken out of commission in 1960 after building a new Ore Preparation Plant and Blast Furnace.

Flixborough Wharf was built to serve Lysaghts Works in switching from rail transport to shipping.

In the period between 1948 and 1952 the whole Steel Plant was remodelled and the Blast Furnace Department enhanced at a cost of nearly £10 million. A rod mill was dismantled at GKN's Castle Works in Wales and re-built at Lysaghts.

On 1 September 1964 steel was produced by the new LD/AC steel furnace. This represented Lysaghts move into oxygen steel making.

In 1976 Lysaghts, Redbourn and Appleby-Frodingham Works merged together. The Coke Ovens closed down in 1980 and the whole works closed down in February 1982.

A bird's eye view of Normanby Park Works.

An aerial view of the works in full production.

Building of the Normanby Park blast furnaces, 1911.

Blast furnace workers at the Normanby Park Works in the early days of production.

The Normanby Park power house. The blowing engines can be seen at the far end.

The Normanby Park melting shop, *c.*1965.

Another view of the Normanby Park melting shop showing the unique charger system, *c.*1965.

The following series of photographs provide a record of the last charge and cast at Normanby Park Works on 25 February 1981. This first picture shows the casting of iron into a torpedo ladle.

The last charge at the LD Plant.

Filling the ingot bowls with the last cast.

A closer view of the process, showing the pit foreman observing the last sample being taken.

The LD steel plant control room for the last cast.

The last day at Normanby Park Rolling Mill. The Rolling Mill shut down a day earlier, on 24 February.

Some of the steel plant maintenance workers on the last day.

Mill workers on their last day at work.

'Last man out, switch off.' An example of gallows humour.

A last look at Normanby Park Works in its heyday, showing the melting shop and blast furnaces.

Five
Appleby Frodingham

The second ironworks in Scunthorpe was Frodingham Ironworks; built by Joseph Cliff in partnership with his son-in-law, William Hirst. The first blast furnace was blown-in in 1865 and was made of brick. The use of brick was probably due to the fact that Joseph Cliff was a brick maker who had a brick works and plumbago (graphite) works at Wortley near Sheffield. In 1871 the original two blast furnaces were re-built using steel and a further two furnaces were added. Joseph Cliff's son, also called Joseph, came to work at Frodingham, while William Hirst left. In 1879, on the death of Joseph Cliff the elder, his five sons, William, Joseph, Philip, Walter and Stephen, became joint owners.

Frodingham was the first works in Scunthorpe to enter into steel making, with the first cast of steel made on 21 March 1890. The steel was made into ingots and fed into a Cogging Mill. The steel furnaces were the open-hearth type and were the first to be used in this country. The first mechanically-charged blast furnace in Europe was built at Frodingham in 1904.

In 1917 the Frodingham Iron & Steel Co. Ltd share capital was sold to Steel Peach & Tozer and Samuel Fox.

Appleby Ironworks was the sixth ironworks to be built and blew-in their first two blast furnaces in 1876 and 1877. They had trouble with their lease and were bankrupted by the coal strike of 1912. Winn offered more favourable terms to Frodingham Iron & Steel Co. Ltd who, in association with the Steel Company of Scotland, accepted the lease. During 1918 the United Steel Companies was formed with Appleby Ironworks shares being bought from the Steel Company of Scotland. At this time, Appleby Ironworks amalgamated with Frodingham but was still run as a separate works until 1934, when the two works merged as the Appleby Frodingham Steel Co. Ltd.

Major developments continued with the new Appleby Melting Shop and Plate Mills coming on stream in 1927, and the building of South Ironworks in 1938, with the new coke ovens being built on the site of the old North Lincoln Ironworks. Further extensions were completed in 1954 when South Ironworks built a new ore preparation plant that included four new sinter strands and an ore bedding plant. It also added two new blast furnaces to the original two.

The steel industry was nationalized in 1967 and, in 1968, the combined works of Redbourn, Lysaghts and Appleby Frodingham became the Scunthorpe Group of the British Steel Corporation.

In 1973 the ANCHOR major development scheme came on stream with basic oxygen steel making, section Mills, bloom and billet Mills and orders placed for continuous casting machines. This eventually brought about the closure of Lysaghts Works in 1981 and the final closure of Redbourn Works in 1988 when the Sinter Plant, which was kept running to feed Queen Mary and Queen Bess Blast Furnaces, closed down.

In March 1987, the Scunthorpe Works of the British Steel Corporation became the first fully integrated steel plant in the world to be awarded third party approval by Lloyd's Register Quality Assurance. In 1988, British Steel plc shares were floated on the stockmarket.

An aerial view of Frodingham Ironworks in the early 1950s.

A view of the Frodingham Iron and Steel Works showing the second town railway station and Station Hotel.

The Frodingham Blowing Engine House.

Quarter-crank blowing engines. Built in 1904, they remained in use for fifty years.

A view of the Frodingham Ironworks looking east (c.1905) showing the quarter-crank blowing engine house.

Frodingham House. The house was knocked down before the building of the 'Yankee' blast furnace in 1905.

Frodingham Iron and Steel Works.

Building of the 'Yankee' blast furnace, the first mechanically-charged blast furnace, 1905. Scunthorpe's first railway station and station-master's house can be seen in front of the furnace.

Frodingham Ironworks shortly after building two additional hand-charged blast furnaces and a central lift tower in 1870.

An aerial view of Frodingham Ironworks and Frodingham Steel Works in the 1920s. The works canteen and main office block can be seen in the foreground.

Frodingham Steel Works shortly after it was built in 1890. The chemical works, which processed slag from the steel works, are visible in the background. This burned down at the turn of the twentieth century.

The first steel furnaces.

The crew that built Frodingham Melting Shop, 1890.

Above and below: Two views of the hand-fed Frodingham 15in Mill.

A view from Chemical Works Corner (*c*.1900) showing the chemical works building on the right, the new Frodingham Melting Shop in the centre and, in the distant left, Frodingham Ironworks.

Ruins of the Chemical Works following its destruction by fire in the early 1900s.

Appleby Ironworks shortly after blowing-in its first furnaces in 1876-1877.

An aerial photo of Appleby Ironworks taken in the 1950s. The hills in the foreground were formed by overburden removal from the redundant Trent ironstone mines. To the right of the gasholder is Santon Terrace and Santon Hostel.

Rebuilding one of
Appleby Ironworks
blast furnaces.

An aerial photo of Appleby Steel Works taken in the 1950s. In the foreground is Appleby canteen, the metallurgy department and the welfare department. The nine chimneys of Frodingham Melting Shop are on the left and the plate Mills buildings on the right.

Following pages: Wellman 4-ton charger charging lime into R steel furnace.

Charging an AJAX steel furnace. It was named after Albert Jackson, the designer.

Charging an AJAX steel furnace, showing the oxygen injection system.

Delivering ingot moulds to Appleby Mills.

Removing ingot moulds.

Loading hot ingot onto the Cogging Mill, 3 February 1958.

Appleby Slabbing Mill, 23 March 1960.

Appleby 7ft Mill cooling bank.

Building South Ironworks, 1938. In particular the erection of Nos .9 and 10 blast furnaces and the building of the blowing engine house can be seen here.

Installation of the M.A.N. German blowing engines, 1938.

The turbo blowers built in 1954 under the SERAPHIM project to replace the 1938 blowing engines.

South Ironworks blast furnaces, after the completion of the SERAPHIM project in 1954. The two furnaces in the background are the 1938 Nos 9 and 10 furnaces and the two nearer furnaces are Nos 11 and 12. The furnaces were then renumbered 1, 2, 3 ,4 before becoming the Four Queens, Mary, Bess, Anne and Victoria. In the foreground is the new sinter material bedding plant.

The new blast furnace cast house in pristine condition shortly after its construction in 1954.

Following pages: APEX sinter plant, the first air-cooled sinter coolers in the country. Redbourn Ironworks can be seen in the background, on the left.

A view of Queen Victoria, looking north to the other Queens.

The new C and D sinter plants built under the SERAPHIM project. These were started simultaneously with the new blast furnaces on 28 July 1954 by Sir Archibald Forbes, Chairman of the Iron and Steel Board.

Queens Mary and Bess Cast House.

An aerial view of South Ironworks after the commissioning of E sinter plant in 1965.
Scunthorpe's tower blocks can be seen in the background.

Hot metal charging at the new Frodingham Melting Shop, South Ironworks.

Inside the Appleby Melting Shop. The people are, from left to right: Harry Cleary (First Hand), Bill Smith (Second Hand), Stan Markham (Charger Driver), Brian Clayton (Assistant Manager), Mick Ridgely (Crane Driver), Roy Leaning (Third Hand), Ray King (Sample Passer).

Back view of the South Smelting Shop.

Front view of the South Smelting Shop.

Building of the new ANCHOR project, 1971.

The Bloom and Billet Mill, final stand and flying shear, in operation. This photograph gives some indication of the length of the building.

Six
At Work

The First and Second Hands looking into a steel furnace. Their experience allowed them to tell, simply by looking, when a furnace was ready for casting.

Roller Boss gauging the thickness of hot plate during the rolling process.

Appleby Sketch Shears, c.1930. These were used to cut the plate

Preparing the pay-packets at Appleby-Frodingham Wages Department.

Thursday was pay-day. Here Appleby workers are collecting their wages. Shift-workers would come in on their day off to collect theirs.

The Joiner's Shop situated in Winn's Corridor.

At a works telephone exchange. The operators also controlled the system of pneumatic tubes used to relay important messages around the works.

Teaching shorthand at the Central Typing Department.

Learning touch-typing. Notice the boxes covering the keyboards used during practice.

Frodingham Sectional Cold Straighteners, *c*.1920.

Plate Layers laying rail track.

Frodingham Roll Turners at the beginning of the twentieth century.

A Roll Turner in the 1950s.

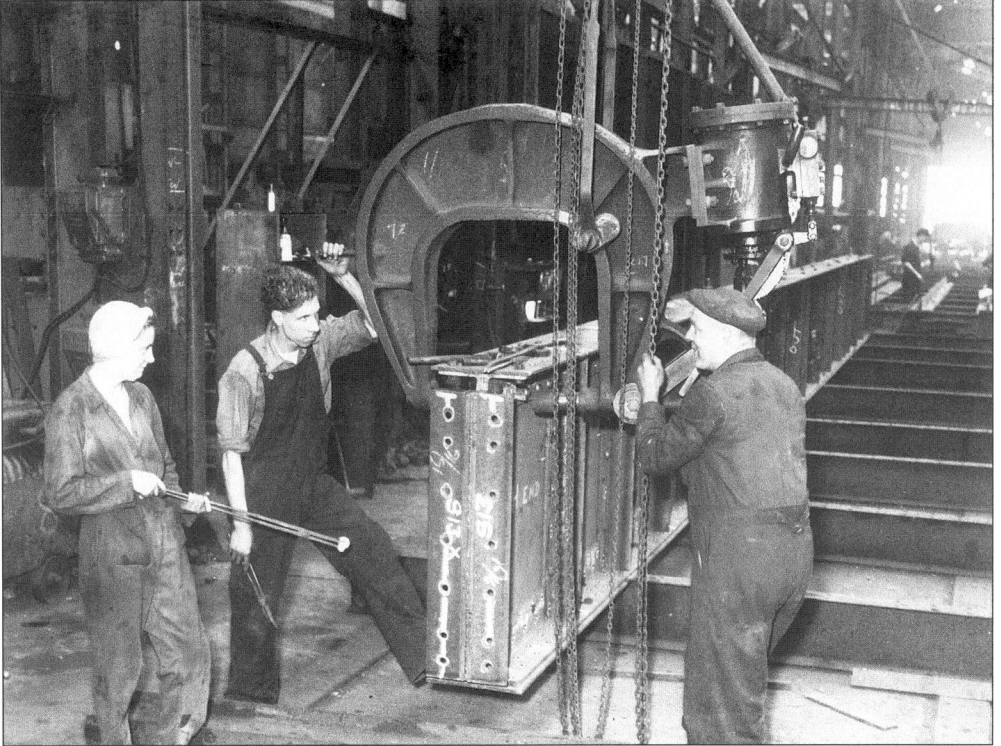

Women in the steel industry. Riveters at work in the construction department.

Loco cleaning.

Appleby-Frodingham Womens Works Council and Safety Sub-Committees. 1956. Left to right, front row: Mrs A.M. Doubtfire, Mrs S.V. Castelow, Mrs S.A Chambers, Miss H. Lewis, Mrs A. Brown, Miss M. Ball, Mrs J. O'Donnell, Mrs D.M. Davey. Back row: Miss D.E. Hind. Mrs J. Austin, Mrs H.W. Richardson, Mrs I. Lawrence, Mrs F. Auckland.

15in Mill Field girls, 1958. Left to right, back row: Mrs D. Wringe, Mrs M. Keneally, Mrs B. Koltac, Mrs J. Cross, Mrs M. Troke, Miss P. Clappison, Miss G. Baxter, Mrs D. McCutcheon. Front row: Miss E. Frow, Miss D. Stainton, Mrs N. Smith, Mrs J. Austin (Welfare Supervisor), Miss R. Vear, Mrs L. Fletcher, Miss J. Osborne.

Norman Donner and George Stibenson filling the charging barrows at North Ironworks.

The last barrow-load for the last cast at No.2 Blast Furnace, Frodingham, 9 January 1950. The man at the back is Tom Seymour, thought to have penned the verse on the furnace.

The last cast at Frodingham No.1 furnace on 17 May 1954. The blast furnace manager is casting the plaques. Lou Sutton, ex- Scunthorpe United winger, is holding the plaque. To his left is Bert Chute and to his right are Jack Clark, Joe Smith and Fred Cooke.

'Nibblem' foundry.

Steam loco removing a slag ladle from the blast furnaces.

Tipping slag south of Chemical Works Corner, on Brigg Road.

The staff of Joseph Cliff & Sons, Frodingham, 1886.

Lysaghts Coke Oven Gang, 1950.

The last day at Normanby Park wet canteen, 13 March 1981.

Leaving work by North Lincoln Road, Appleby Works junction.

Seven

Events

Front cover of a special illuminated address, presented to the Hon. Roland Winn on the occasion of his 21st birthday.

The Lincolnshire Ironmaster's Association, comprising the following companies:

The Appleby Iron Company, Limited,
The Frodingham Iron and Steel Company, Limited,
The North Lincolnshire Iron Company, Limited,
The Redbourn Hill Iron and Coal Company, Limited, and
The Trent Iron Company, Limited,

representing the important Iron and Steel under-takings carried on upon Lord St. Oswald's estate in Lincolnshire, desire to tender to you very sincere and heartfelt congratulations on the occasion of your twenty-first birthday.

It may be interesting to you to know that the industry we represent was established in the year 1860 and that it has involved a capital expenditure of more than £1,000,000 and now finds employment for about 4,000 workpeople.

It was established in the time of your great grandfather and many of us remember with affection and gratitude the great personal interest which your grandfather took in the many difficulties which attended the inauguration of the industry in its early days.

Above and opposite: The text pages of the illuminated address.

The kindly relations thus begun have been maintained and strengthened by your father, and we rejoice to be able very respectfully to join in the feelings of happiness and pleasure which this interesting event will occasion to Lady St. Oswald and his Lordship.

You are the descendant of a family which possesses a noble history of public service and we feel sure that the records of your ancestors will inspire you to a life of devotion to the best interests of your King and your country.

Our heartfelt prayer is that the bright prospect before you may be fully realised and that in the years to come you may be able to look back upon your life with satisfaction equal to the hope we now have for your future.

The Appleby Iron Company, Limited,

The Frodingham Iron and Steel Company, Limited,

The North Lincolnshire Iron Company, Limited,

The Redbourn Hill Iron and Coal Company, Limited, and

The Trent Iron Company, Limited.

The Winn family portraits from the illuminated address.

A series of views of the local ironworks, which conclude the address.

Section of the plate rolled by H.R.H. Prince George on 26 October 1923 on a visit to the Appleby Works.

Queen Elizabeth on her visit to Normanby Park Works in July 1940. Mr Gough, Chief Engineer, is on her left, and Mr E.C. Lysaght is on her right. The Guard of Honour second from the left is Mr J. Firth.

Visit of the Queen and Prince Philip, June 1958. Lt Cdr G.W. Wells is pointing out details of one of the working models.

The visit of the Queen to the ANCHOR site in 1974. Angela Cooke, standing in the background, has just presented her with her bouquet.

The visit of the Mayor of Scunthorpe, Cllr Clarence Newlove, and his guests to the Appleby-Frodingham Steel Company in September 1954.

Sir Archibald Forbes, Chairman of the Iron and Steel Board, starting up the SERAPHIM Plant on 29 July 1954. On the left is G.D. Elliot and on the right is Lt Cdr Wells.

A visit of retired employees to Frodingham Ironworks, *c.*1937. Among them are: Ted Eake (NUB District Secretary), Tommy Cook (Blast Furnace Foreman), A. Wolverson (NUB Delegate), Tom Mitchell (Assistant Manager), C.A.J. Behrendt (Blast Furnace Manager), Frank Lawson (Blast Furnace Foreman), George Catt (Bricklayer Foreman), Len Jessop (Hoist Driver).

Visit of the British Iron and Steel Board to Redbourn Works, *c.* 1964.

Mr E.C. Lysaght, grandson of the founder, with some of his staff.

Lysaght's office staff, 1922. Left to right, back row: Geo. Piercy, Edwin Buttrick, Frank Graser, Cyril Johnson, S. Hornsby, W. Osgerby, Lewis Adsetts. Second row: Joe Parrot, Kenneth Jehu, John Green, Mr Reynolds, Charles Beacock, Florence Barton, Fred Hallam, Lillian Martin, John Murray, Evelyn Manton, Tom Woffenden, Max Haresign, Herbert Frost, Herbert East, William Ansell, R.S. Phillips, Enoch Markham, Mr West, William Booth. Front row: William Richardson, E. Phelps, Edwin Pittwood, Sam Bennett, Elijah Dicks, R.S. Williams, Walter Beverley, Wilfred Holmes, Mr Wilkinson, A.C. Ashmore, Percy Benn, Arthur Pool.

Appleby Frodingham Plate Mills football team, c.1926.

Christmas Day Broadcast participants from South Ironworks, 1949. Stan Whiting, S. Spence and H. Jessop. The other man is unknown.

Union officials gathered at the retirement of Fred Cooke, holding the glass. From left to right, front row: Ken Stones, Les Bramley, Frank Bradley, Fred Cooke, Peter Whyte, John Willsmore. Second row: Terry King, Fred Ward, Bob Haggerty, Cyril Starkey, Gordon Slingsby, Dave Keenan, Roger Jenman. Back row: Dave Crowther, Peter Hoyle, Sam Pearson, Jeff Lonsdale, John McNeil, Kevin Ringrose, Mike Collins, Norman Grant, Barry Nainby, Norman Jupp, David Geary.

The visit of William and Andrew Clarkson, the grandson and great-grandson of Maxmilian Mannaberg, 7 August 1989. Left to right: Mike Bowness, Reg Cooke, Andrew Clarkson, John H Craig, William Clarkson, Keith Graham, Derek Bains.

A friendly ceremony at Brumby Hall when Harry Hinchcliffe, the groundsman, said his final farewell at the age of seventy-eight.

The first Appleby-Frodingham Children's Gala Committee at Brumby Hall, 1929.

The Children's Gala queen and princesses at Brumby Hall, 8 June 1963.

Cllr Eric Arnold, Mayor of Scunthorpe, with the prizewinners at the Children's Gala in 1977.

Faces at the Punch and Judy, Appleby-Frodingham Gala 1977.

More happy faces at the 1972 Gala.

Enjoying the ride at the Normanby Park Gala 1978.

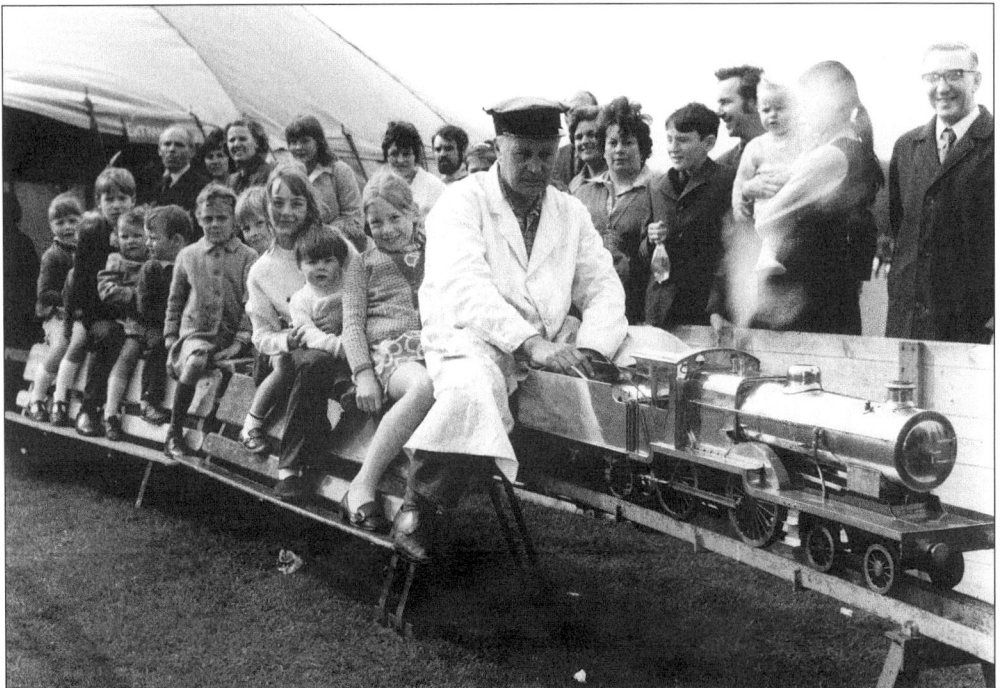

More riders, from the 1972 Appleby-Frodingham Gala.

Police and pickets outside Frodingham Steel Works, Brigg Road, during the strike of 1909.

The strike of contractors working on the SERAPHIM site in 1953. The three men on the platform are, from left to right: Jack Stanley, General Secretary of the CEU, Paddy Bransfield, Senior Steward, and George Booth, Sheffield area representative of the CEU.

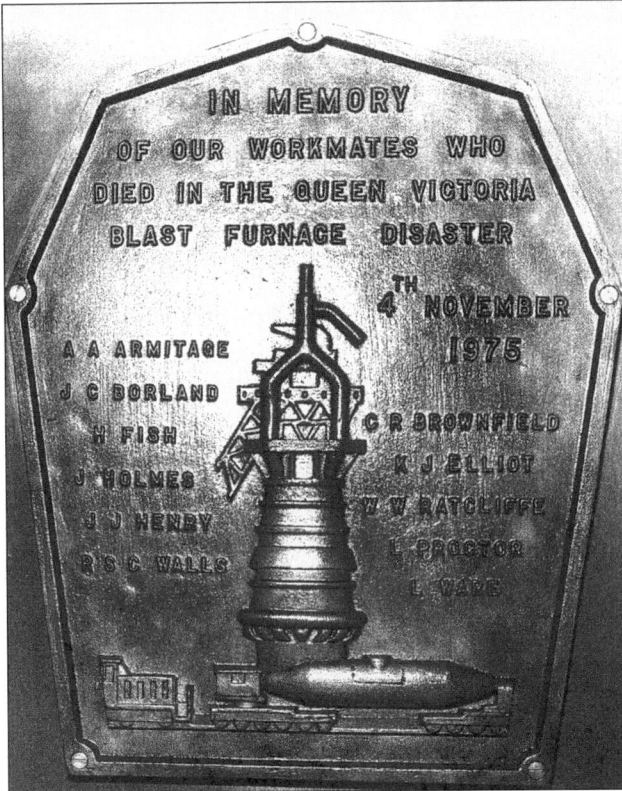

The plaque at the Four Queens blast furnaces in memory of the following people who lost their lives in the Queen Victoria blast furnace disaster on 4 November 1975: A.A. Armitage, J.C. Borland, H. Fish, J. Holmes, J.J. Henry, R.S.C. Walls, C.R. Brownfield, K.J. Elliot, W.W. Ratcliffe, L. Proctor and L. Ware.

The NYPRO chemical plant disaster at Flixborough, 1 June 1974.

Eight

Scunthorpe –the Worker's Town

Scunthorpe High Street viewed from Home Street. Fletcher's Chemist is on the left and, in the distance, the Blue Bell Hotel can be seen in the middle.

Harvey's Transport loaded with steel piling.

Clugston Cawood lorry outside the public baths.

Johnny Green's tobacconist and Fowler's drapers, lower High Street.

Mr and Mrs Westaby and their son outside their newsagents, opposite Green's tobacconists.

Junction of High Street and Market Hill, with Melia's on the corner.

George Howson, fish and fruit merchant, High Street.

Robinson's Ironmongers, at the corner of Belgrave Square and High Street. In their early days they supplied the blasting powder used by miners.

Heslam's Furniture Store, which was converted from the old Primitive Methodist Chapel. Above are the tax offices.

The Dine's Fish & Chip Restaurant, which was open throughout most of the 1920s and later became Peacock's Penny Bazaar and then the *Palais de Dance*. During the Second World War it became Scunthorpe Public Library.

Scunthorpe Fish Merchants, situated between Gilliat Street and Frances Street.

Callister's Bread Shop on the south side of the High Street, just beyond the Oswald Hotel.

Inside Cribb's Fishmongers, at No.198 Ashby High Street, showing Bromley's Grocers and Smith's Butchers on the opposite side of the road. On Good Friday, Cribb's were open from 4.30 a.m. in order to supply the shift workers with fish, and they usually closed around 3 p.m., having sold one and a half tons of fish.

Bradley's Clothiers.

Roland Franklin Ladies and Gents Outfitters, Ashby High Street.

British Legion band preparing to play at a 1920s hospital carnival.

Joint meeting of the Scunthorpe Rotary and Scunthorpe 1968 Probus Clubs, in May 1993. From left to right, front row: Reg Tindall, Tom Cribb, Ron Simpson, and Derek Baxter. Back row: Bill Hesketh, Edwin Dowse, Ken Heath, Gordon Wilson, Ron Everett, Harry Harcock. These men could look back upon a lifetime of service to the town, its trade and its industry.

Scunthorpe and District Rifle club friendly match. Dr Behrendt's Team *v.* Mr Kiddle's team, 27 June 1915.

Bowling competition teams on the bowling green at the corner of Fenton Street and Cole Street, now a car park.

Station Hotel, which was opposite Frodingham Ironworks.

Scunthorpe public swimming and slipper baths.

The Palace Theatre in Cole Street, with the Salvation Army Citadel further along the road.

Harold Cryer on the organ at the Ritz Cinema.

Blessing of the new St John's Church vicarage at Normanby Road, 1950, built on the south section of the site of the old vicarage, now The Hollies. From left to right, front row: Revd John Swaby, Vicar of St John's Church, Bishop Greaves of Grimsby, Canon Greason of Frodingham Church. Back row: Emlyn Williams and Cyril Dobson, Church Wardens.

Frodingham Church interior, before its extension in 1913.

Primitive Methodist Centenary Church, Frodingham Road, Scunthorpe. It was burnt down in 1970.

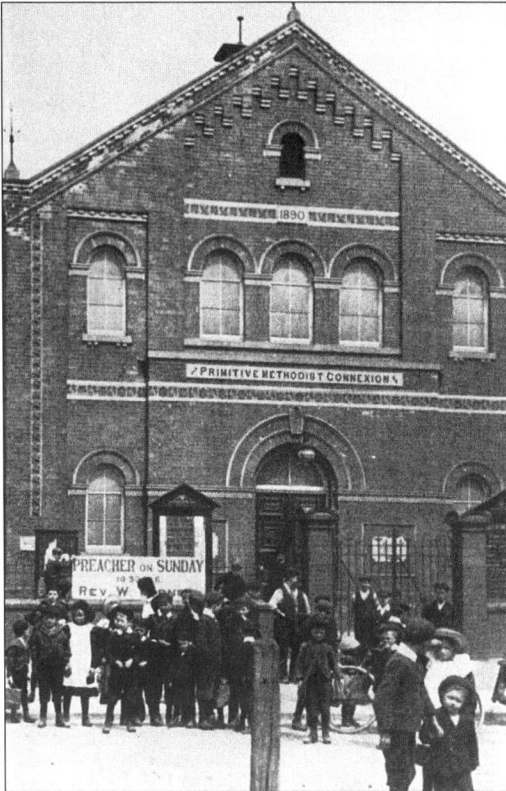

The Primitive Methodist Chapel, which later became Heslam House. Woolworth's now stands on the site in the High Street.

A brief chronology of Scunthorpe's iron and steel industry

200 Million Years BC
During the Lower Jurassic Period Frodingham Ironstone iss deposited over a period of three to four million years.

2,500 BC
Iron Age begins on a small scale in the Middle East.

1400 BC
Iron Age begins in Anatola when a larger scale way of smelting was found.

1000 BC
The Iron Age spreads across Europe and iron tools and weapons become more widespread.

500 BC
Celts bring the Iron Age to Britain.

AD 43
Roman occupation of Britain. The small and scattered iron industry, mainly in the Sussex and Surrey area, is expanded.

1496
The first blast furnace in Britain is erected at Newbridge, Sussex. It was developed near Liège, Belgium.

1709
Abraham Darby converts a small charcoal furnace to use coke.

1856
Bessimer invents the process of blowing cold air through molten iron.

1857
Mr Clarke gives his business interests in Bristol to his friend John Lysaght.

1859
The re-discovery of the Frodingham ironstone bed by a shooting party led by Charles Winn, on his land east of Scunthorpe.

1860
July: First iron ore mined in Scunthorpe area. Commencement of railway construction to link the existing railway, up to Keadby, with the railway at Barnetby.

1861
Narrow gauge railway constructed to transport ore from Dawes Brothers mines to the new wharf at Gunness.

1862
Commencement of the building of Dawes Brothers Trent Ironworks, the first ironworks in Scunthorpe.

1863
Creation of the Frodingham Iron Co.

1864
Building of Frodingham Works begins. The first blast furnace is completed in May. On 26 March Trent Ironworks casts its first iron. On 2 October the second furnace at Trent is blown-in. Railway construction completed.

1865
May: Frodingham Iron Co. first furnace blown-in with local ore and Durham ore. No.1 Furnace at Frodingham works wrecked by explosion.

1866
The third ironworks, North Lincoln Ironworks, built. The first furnace is blown-in in May. In September one of its furnaces blows up, leading to doubts about closed-top furnaces.

1867
Open-topped furnaces introduced at the two Frodingham Blast Furnaces.

1869
The British Iron & Steel Institute formed.

1870
Two more blast furnaces added at Frodingham. The first underground mineshafts are sunk about this time.

1871
North Lincoln Ironworks blow-in their second Blast Furnace.

1872
Two small hand-charged Blast Furnaces come into operation at the Redbourn Hill Iron & Coal Co.

1873
The Lincolnshire Iron & Smelting Co. Works start production.

1874
Appleby Iron Co. formed.

1875
North Lincoln Works build a further two blast furnaces.

1876
Appleby Ironworks blow-in their first blast furnace.

1877
Appleby Ironworks blow-in their second Blast Furnace.

1879
Joseph Cliff dies and leaves Frodingham Ironworks to his five sons.

1880
Redbourn Hill Iron and Coal Company's third blast furnace blown-in.

1882
Ironstone workings between New Frodingham village and Brigg Road worked out.

1883
The Lincolnshire Iron & Smelting Co. run into financial difficulties, are purchased by the Redbourn Hill Iron & Coal Co. and are re-named Lindsey Ironworks, but are not used and fall into disrepair.

1885
In 1885 or 1886, the small Foundry near Trent Works, known locally as 'Nibblem Clink', is acquired by Frodingham Ironworks.

1886
The British Iron & Steel and Kindred Trades Confederation (BISAKTA) established.

1887
A larger railway station opened to replace the original one opened in 1866. The Station Hotel also opened.

1888
First discussions at Frodingham Ironworks on the possibilities of steelmaking. The Cliff brothers decided to build a steelmaking plant.

1890
21 March: The first steel to be cast in Scunthorpe from the Frodingham Steel Works.

1892
January: Formation of the Lincolnshire Ironmasters Association and formation of the National Federation of Blastfurnacemen.

1895
A 14in Mill built at Frodingham Works. It was later altered to 15in.

1897
First trials with Mr Thwaites' small gas blowing engine at Frodingham.

1898
F Furnace added at Frodingham Steelworks.

1899
G Furnace added at Frodingham Steelworks.

1900
Gas lighting superseded by electric lighting at Frodingham Works. Electric power also extensively installed.

1901
The original A & B steel furnaces were demolished and H furnace put into operation at Frodingham about this time.

1902
The first Talbot tilting steel furnace goes into production.

1904
Frodingham Iron & Steel Co. becomes a limited company. Work commences on building a new No.4 Blast Furnace at Frodingham. It will become known as 'The Yankee'.

1905
Lindsey Ironworks demolished.

1906
Redbourn Hill Iron & Coal Co. acquired by Clumfelin Steel & Tinplate Co.

1907
A lawsuit takes place between Appleby Iron Co. and Lord St Oswald's mines over ore supply. It is after this that the decline of Appleby Iron Co. begins.

1908
At Frodingham second blowing engine house built, No.1 Blast Furnace demolished.

1909
Redbourn Hill Iron & Coal Co. build a third blast furnace. 15 April to 10 May: Scunthorpe Steel strike.

1910
Site clearing commences for the building of John Lysaght's Normanby Park Iron & Steel Works.

1911
Work begins on the erection of John Lysaght's Normanby Park Iron & Steel Works. Frodingham begins building a new soaker building.

1912
Normanby Park Works' three blast furnaces blown-in and production started. The

National Coal Strike bankrupts the Appleby Iron Co. They go into liquidation on 5 May, and in June the Frodingham Iron & Steel Co. in partnership with the Steel Co. of Scotland, takes the works over and the Appleby blast furnaces are restarted on 22 June. No.1 blast furnace at Frodingham is rebuilt. The Iron & Steel Institute visit Frodingham Iron & Steel Co. Ltd.

1913
Eight hour shifts introduced at Frodingham Works.

1914
Outbreak of the First World War. War demand for more steel creates major developments and more mechanization in the mines. Fourth blast furnace built at Normanby Park Works.

1915
Ministry of Munitions set up. All Scunthorpe works are geared to war production.

1916
Redbourn Works build a fourth blast furnace along with coke ovens, steel furnaces and rolling mills. A new road/rail bridge is built over the River Trent, alongside the old rail bridge.

1917
The control of Redbourn Hill Iron & Coal Co. is taken over by Richard Thomas & Co. (later Richard Thomas & Baldwins). Appleby starts work on Nos 5 and 6 Blast Furnaces. The Steel Co. of Scotland drop out of their partnership in Appleby Iron Co.

1918
Armistice: 12 to 15 November all furnaces at Appleby and Frodingham damped down for holidays to celebrate the end of the war. Appleby-Frodingham Works Athletic Club formed. The three-shift system brought in for the first time. Appleby Iron Co. is bought out and merged with Frodingham Iron & Steel Co. Ltd to become Appleby-Frodingham Iron & Steel Co. Ltd.

1919
Scunthorpe and Frodingham joined as an urban district. John Lysaght's interests are sold to the Berry Group.

1920
June: Guest, Keen & Nettleford's buy John Lysaght's Normanby Park Works from the Berry Group, and a fifth blast furnace is added.

1921
The worst year in the history of iron and steel production. January 1921 to January 1923: all Appleby Blast Furnaces shut down. 27 March to 4 August: all Frodingham furnaces shut down. Normanby Park Works close down. Between 1921 and 1933 Redbourn works close down on a number of occasions due to the Depression. The first meeting of the executive of the completely Amalgamated Union of Blastfurnacemen, Ore Miners, Coke Workers and Kindred Trades.

1922
North Lincoln Ironworks purchased by Stewart & Lloyds.

1924
The firm of Redbourn is liquidated. Redbourn Works close in the summer. 5 June: No.1 Blast Furnace at Appleby blown-out. This is the first Appleby-Frodingham blast furnace to become redundant.

1925
February: the Redbourn Hill Iron & Coal Co. Ltd is wound up.

1926
2 May: Coal and General Strike, furnaces at Appleby-Frodingham damped down for thirty-five weeks.

1927
A new Appleby Blast Furnace (No.5) is blown-in on 20 January. 10 September, Appleby's No.2 Blast Furnace blown-out for the last time. Appleby-Frodingham Safety First Committee formed.

1928
November: Redbourn's blast furnaces back in operation after shutdown for bad trading figures.

1930
Normanby Park Works build a new battery of coke ovens, the first of its kind in the country. North Lincoln Ironworks comes to a standstill. A fourth steel furnace is added at Appleby Steelworks. January: Appleby-Frodingham Works Benevolent Fund constituted. June: the works first gasholder built at Appleby.

1931
Appleby's Nos1 and 2 Blast Furnaces demolished.

1932
Appleby-Frodingham, 10 July: Two Pan Greenawalt Sinter Plant ordered for Appleby ironworks. This is the first sinter plant in the U.K. and only the second in Europe. No.4 Blast Furnace at Frodingham blown-in after reconstruction.

1934
The Appleby and Frodingham Works fully amalgamated to become the Appleby Frodingham Steel Co. Ltd. Formation of the British Iron & Steel Federation. 16 June: sinter production starts at Appleby Ironworks.

1935
Trent Ironworks scrapped.

1937
1 January: BISAKTA conclude a national agreement that the working week is reduced from fifty-six to forty-eight hours, inclusive of short meal breaks. June: Site work started on the South Ironworks. August: Orders placed for two blast furnaces to be built on the site. Formation of the British Iron & Steel Control.

1938
North Lincolnshire Ironworks completely demolished. Frodingham Ironstone Mines started a drift mine near Appleby

Ironworks. Around this time Appleby Ironworks becomes known as the North Ironworks of Appleby Frodingham (NIW).

1939
First underground Drift Mine of Frodingham Ironstone Mines opened. Appleby Frodingham: South Ironworks begins production. 3 September: Outbreak of the Second World War. Normanby Park Works geared to war production.

1940
Women become a major workforce as more men are called up. 1 August: Their Majesties King George VI and Queen Elizabeth make a short, surprise, wartime stop and visit Normanby Park and Appleby Frodingham.

1944
26 March: No.1 Blast Furnace at South Ironworks blown-in. December: No.3 Blast Furnace at Frodingham Ironworks blown-out for the last time.

1945
May: War in Europe over. August: War in Japan over.

1946
September: The Iron & Steel Board formed.

1947
November: First steel produced in the new Frodingham (SIW) Melting Shop.

1948
May: The Appleby Frodingham Central Engineering Workshops opened. 17-18 November: Iron and Steel Bill (Nationalization) given its first reading in Parliament.

1949
5 April: No.6 Blast Furnace at North Ironworks blown-in. Bill to nationalize steel is finally law but is delayed in 1950 after the General Election. The Iron & Steel Board is dissolved voluntarily prior to nationalization.

1950
The Schuman Plan for unified control of steel in Europe is announced. 9 January: No.2 Blast Furnace at Frodingham is blown-out for the last time. 27 February: No.5 Blast Furnace at North Ironworks is blown-out.

1951
Normanby Park: A scrap handling plant is built at the Steelworks. Redbourn: The last of the old hand-charged blast furnaces is demolished to make way for the No.2 Blast Furnace. February: Collapse of the foundation of No.5 Blast Furnace at North ironworks. December: Site work on the SERAPHIM project starts.

1952
1 June: Working week reduced from forty-eight to forty-four hours per week without reduction in wages. A further increase in paid holidays from thirteen to eighteen days is agreed. 23 November: No.8 Blast Furnace at North Ironworks blown-out for the last time.

1953
Normanby Park expansion completed. 30 August: No.7 Blast Furnace at North Ironworks blown-out for the last time.

1954
Appleby Frodingham Works see the conclusion of the South Ironworks SERAPHIM project. The old 1938 No.9 and No.10 Blast Furnaces along with the new No.11 and No.12 Blast Furnaces are renumbered Nos 1, 2, 3 and 4 for a short time only and then become The Four Queens – Mary, Bess, Anne and Victoria. Queen Bess was named after Good Queen Bess as it could not be named after a reigning monarch. 16 February: No.5 Blast Furnace at North Ironworks blown-in. 25 February: No.4 Blast Furnace at Frodingham blown-out for the last time. 7 May: No.1 Blast Furnace at Frodingham blown-out for the last time. 10 July: Last sinter made at the Greenawalt Plant at North Ironworks. No.6 Blast Furnace at North Ironworks blown-out for the last time. 1 September: No.5 Blast

Furnace at North Ironworks blown-out for the last time.

1956
Redbourn introduce diesel locomotives. Redbourn Apprentice Training Centre opened.

1958
Winterton Quarry opened up to supply ironstone to Redbourn Works. The first stone is mined in 1959. 27 June: The Visit to Appleby Frodingham of HM the Queen and Prince Philip, the Duke of Edinburgh. May: introduction of the forty-two-hour working week.

1960
Normanby Park Works: Greenwalt Sinter Plant taken out of commission.

1967
22 March: Nationalization of the steel industry. 22 July: British Steel Co. formed under the chairmanship of Lord Melchett. One of the first acts of the British Steel Co. is to give the 'go ahead' for the ANCHOR development.

1968
A government white paper recommends that the British iron and steel Industry be rationalized into five main areas. Scunthorpe is to be one of those areas.

1969
Appleby Frodingham Works, ANCHOR Project given approval.

1970
20 March: the Lincolnshire Ironmasters Association dissolved. April: the Scunthorpe Group of Works joins the newly formed General Steels Division of the British Steel Co.

1971
January: Normanby Park Works, open-hearth steel making ended. July: Redbourn Works, closure of the Rolling Mill. 22 February: Queen Bess Blast Furnace dust-catcher explodes during a blow-down ready

for furnace rebuild. No one is severely injured.

1973
Redbourn and Appleby Frodingham Works merge under the ANCHOR Scheme.

1974
February: steelmaking stops at Redbourn. 6 May: Her Majesty the Queen and Prince Philip visit the ANCHOR development. Saturday 1 June: NYPRO chemical plant at Flixborough explodes.

1975
May: Normanby Park Works Rod Mill closes. June: Appleby Frodingham Slab Mill Closes. 4 November: water runs onto a torpedo ladle full of molten iron at Queen Victoria Blast Furnace, causing an explosion of molten metal. Eleven people are killed.

1976
Normanby Park Works merge with Redbourn Works and Appleby Frodingham Works.

1980
January: coke making at Redbourn Works ceases. May: Santon Mines close down. June: Normanby Park Works Coke Ovens close down. August: Winterton Mines shut down. 8 September: the last of Redbourn's blast furnaces blown up and demolished. A national steel strike lasts for thirteen weeks.

1981
February: Normanby Park Works close down after sixty-nine years.

1984
12 March: National Union of Mineworkers strike. It lasted fifty-two weeks. Normanby Park Reclamation Scheme started.

1985
May to September: Queen Mary Blast Furnace completely rebuilt. Appleby Frodingham Works move from the Midland Division of the British Steel Co. into the General Steels Division and are renamed

the Scunthorpe Works of B.S.C. The name of Appleby Frodingham is then phased out.

1987
March: Scunthorpe Works of British Steel becomes the first fully integrated steelworks in the world to be awarded third party approval by Lloyds Register Quality Assurance.

1988
23 November: British Steel Shares flotation date to become a private company. December: British Steel becomes British Steel plc. December: local ore mining stops. December: Redbourn Sinter Plant completely closed down. Between 1970 and 1988 over 13,000 jobs have been lost in the Scunthorpe iron and steel Industry.

1989
July: Dock strike. It lasts nine weeks.

1990
21 March: Centenary of steelmaking at Scunthorpe. 23 May: Queen Anne Blast Furnace off for a complete rebuild.

Bibliography

Books

H.S. Ayres, *100 Years of Iron-making at Appleby-Frodingham*
P.F. Bell, *A Short History of Redbourn Ironworks*
R. Cooke, *History of Burden Preparation*
R. Cooke, *Men of Iron, Men of Steel, A Celebration of 100 Years of Steelmaking in Scunthorpe*
R. & K. Cooke, *The Archive Photograph Series – Scunthorpe*
H. Dudley, *History of Scunthorpe & Frodingham*
J. Owen, *Ironmen – A Short Study of the History of the Union from 1878 to 1953* (BISAKTA)
Scunthorpe Co-operative Society, *Jubilee History, 1874-1924*
GR Walshaw & CAJ Behrendt, *History of Appleby Frodingham*
J. Vaizey, *The History of British Steel*

Reports and articles

Appleby-Frodingham Steel Co., *South Ironworks*
GKN Group, *Lysaghts, Scunthorpe*
British Steel Smelters Report, 1909
'Verbatim Report of an Interview with Talbot Cliff to J.G. Clugston', transcribed by W. Bennington
'Technical Survey of the Iron & Steel Works of Appleby-Frodingham', *Iron & Coal Trades Review*
'Technical Survey of Richard, Thomas & Baldwins Group', *Iron & Coal Trades Review*.
'Lysaghts Scunthorpe Works', *Steel Times*, 5 March 1965
Appleby-Frodingham Chronicle (various editions and writers)
Appleby-Frodingham News (various editions and writers)
Scunthorpe Evening Telegraph (various editions and writers)

A view from St John's Church Tower, looking towards the Four Queens.